Author: Elliot Harrison
ISBN HARDBACK: 978-9916-88-894-0
ISBN PAPERBACK: 978-9916-88-895-7

The Solace of the Silent Deep

In shadows where the waters breathe,
The whispers of the calm unite,
A gentle sigh, a peaceful wreath,
In depths where day dissolves to night.

A cradle made of sapphire hue,
Where silver fish in silence glide,
Amidst the dreams that drift in blue,
The secrets of the deep abide.

The quiet lulls the restless mind,
With every wave that hugs the shore,
A refuge for the lost and blind,
A balm that heals forevermore.

Beneath the surface, time stands still,
With echoes soft that gently sweep,
In tranquil depths, there lies a will,
To find the solace of the deep.

Conch Shells Whispering Memories

In twilight hues the conch shells lay,
Their whispers soft, a time's ballet.
Secrets of the sea, they softly share,
Of distant shores and lovers' care.

Echoes call from ancient tides,
Woven tales where longing hides.
In the grasp of night they sing,
A haunting tune that memories bring.

The Dance of Dust and Water

Particles swirl in the golden light,
A graceful dance, an ethereal sight.
Water droplets play, cascading free,
Painting dreams on what will be.

Each movement tells a silent tale,
Of rivers wide and winds that wail.
Together they weave a timeless thread,
In nature's arms, where moments spread.

Breathing in the Ocean's Embrace

Waves roll gently, a rhythmic sigh,
Breathing softly, the sea draws nigh.
Salt-kissed air, a lover's breath,
Whispers of life and hints of death.

With every tide, a new refrain,
Songs of joy, and hints of pain.
In the swell of water's grace,
We find our home, our truest place.

Resounding Echoes of Longing

In the silence, a deep refrain,
A heart's whisper, a soul's domain.
Fading shadows, lost in time,
Love lingers long, with every rhyme.

Through valleys wide, and mountains steep,
Echoes call from dreams we keep.
These resounding notes through night and day,
Guide us gently, show the way.

Constellations of Sentiment

In the night sky dreams take flight,
Stars whisper secrets, lost in light.
Hearts connect with every gleam,
Painting love in the night's bright theme.

Galaxies swirl in tender grace,
Each twinkle a familiar face.
Through vastness, emotions align,
Constellations of joy entwine.

Echoes of laughter fill the air,
Memories dance, free from despair.
With every glance, hearts dive deep,
Guardians of secrets we keep.

Under the canopy, shadows play,
We find our way, come what may.
In the arms of the soothing night,
Our souls merge in gentle light.

A Symphony of Swells

Waves crash softly on the shore,
A melody that we adore.
Rhythms pulse, a soothing beat,
Nature's song, pure and sweet.

Wind carries whispers through the trees,
Notes entwined with the summer breeze.
Each swell tells a story true,
A symphony composed for two.

Footprints fade as the tide will rise,
In every swell, a new surprise.
Harmony in chaos found,
Love emerges from the sound.

Under the moon, the world will sway,
Dancing dreams in the dusk's soft gray.
Together, we'll ride each swell,
In this ocean where we dwell.

Sailboats of Solitude

Drifting gently on quiet seas,
Sailboats dance with the evening breeze.
Alone yet free, they seek the heart,
Navigating solitude as art.

Stars reflect on the water's face,
A tranquil world, a sacred space.
Each vessel holds its quiet tale,
Of hopes and dreams that never pale.

In the stillness, whispers bloom,
Carried softly, dispelling gloom.
Seeking horizons, they glide anew,
Sailboats of solitude, strong and true.

With every gust, they find their way,
Guided by starlight's gentle ray.
In their journey, peace aligns,
In solitude, their spirit shines.

Moonlit Moods

Under the gaze of the silver moon,
Night wraps us gently, a quiet tune.
Soft shadows dance in whispers light,
Moonlit moods guide hearts through night.

Dreams unravel like threads of gold,
In the stillness, stories unfold.
Every sigh echoes the calm,
Carried forth like a soothing balm.

The world sleeps while wanderers roam,
Finding solace beneath twilight's dome.
In the embrace of the night's soft kiss,
Each moment a fleeting bliss.

With stars above as our host,
We'll cherish this quiet coast.
In moonlit moods, we come alive,
Through the night, our spirits thrive.

A Secret Harbor of Hidden Wounds

In shadows deep, where whispers lie,
A sanctuary of ache and sigh.
The tides that ebb, they hide the scars,
Within the silence, beneath the stars.

Cloaked in the night, the pain retreats,
Among the waves, where heartache meets.
Anchored dreams in a boat of fears,
They drift along with unshed tears.

The Drowning of Silent Sorrows

Beneath the waves, the silence reigns,
Where echoes linger, tied with chains.
Fading voices, lost in despair,
Caught in the depths, gasping for air.

In the ocean's heart, secrets swell,
Stories untold, like a forgotten spell.
A tempest brews, emotions clash,
In darkened waters, shadows flash.

Beneath the Surface, Currents Swirl

A restless tide beneath the calm,
A beckoning touch, a soothing balm.
Underneath, where feelings collide,
The deepest currents, we cannot hide.

Whispers of fate, they weave and twine,
Entangled thoughts, a fragile line.
Beneath the surface, truth awaits,
A mirrored soul, that time creates.

Embracing the Storm Within

Thunder drums in a heart of glass,
Each lightning flash, the moments pass.
The tempest swells, breaking the mold,
A fierce embrace, both brave and bold.

In chaos found, we learn to see,
The strength in vulnerability.
As rain cascades and winds will wail,
We stand as one, through every gale.

Swirling Currents

In the depths where shadows play,
The waters dance and sway.
Whispers of the ocean call,
Secrets held within the thrall.

Ripples weave a tale untold,
Of dreams and nights so bold.
Each swirl a fleeting thought,
In the currents, hope is sought.

Reflections in the moonlit tide,
Where currents pull and glide.
Life flows in endless streams,
A journey born of quiet dreams.

Breaking Barriers

With each step, the walls fall down,
A heart adorned with strength, not crown.
Courage carved in every stride,
A fire within, no need to hide.

Voices rise to shatter skies,
Dreams ignited, spirits rise.
Together we will forge a path,
In unity, we face the wrath.

Limits vanish like morning fog,
Through the struggle, we will slog.
Each moment, bold and fierce,
The future's song, let's hear it pierce.

Horizon of Hopes

At dawn, the sky begins to glow,
A palette of dreams set afloat.
Each hue whispers of new starts,
Promises painted on hopeful hearts.

Across the waves, the sun does rise,
Mirrored in the ocean's eyes.
With every pulse, the future calls,
In its embrace, our spirit sprawls.

To the horizon, we lay our sights,
Chasing warmth of golden lights.
With open arms, we greet the day,
In the journey, we find our way.

The Softest Ripples

A pebble dropped in stillness, clear,
Creates a dance, both bold and sheer.
Gentle waves of love they send,
Through the quiet, they extend.

In softest whispers of the stream,
Echoes of a tender dream.
Each ripple holds a silent word,
In moments shared, emotions stirred.

Caresses of the evening breeze,
In each sigh, the heart finds ease.
Nature sings a lullaby,
In the ripples, we find the why.

Shadows Cast by Turbulent Seas

Beneath the sky, dark whispers roam,
Waves crash loudly, far from home.
Ghostly shadows dance on the deep,
Secrets of the ocean, forever to keep.

Stormy winds, their stories weave,
In the tempest's heart, what do we believe?
The sea's embrace, both fierce and free,
Shadows twist and turn, wild and carefree.

Lullabies of Driftwood and Foam

Gentle waves hum a soft tune,
Under the gaze of the silver moon.
Driftwood whispers tales of yore,
Among the froth, memories soar.

The ocean's sigh, a lullaby sweet,
Cradles the shore in rhythmic beat.
Foam kisses sand, with tender grace,
In this stillness, the world finds its place.

Footprints in the Softest Sand

Quietly walking, with bare feet bare,
Each step a story, written in air.
Footprints fade with the tide's embrace,
Lost in the whispers of time and space.

The warmth of sun warms the land,
As waves gently steal, then expand.
Echoes linger, but soon they're gone,
In the softest sand, life moves on.

Captured in the Moment's Tide

Time stands still on this sandy shore,
With every wave, memories roar.
Captured moments, like shells on the land,
Glimmers of life, held in our hands.

The tide pulls back, revealing the past,
Whispers of each moment, fading fast.
Yet in this space, we pause and reflect,
A journey of heart, we deeply connect.

A Mosaic of Shifting Emotions

In the morning, joy takes flight,
Colors dance in soft daylight.
Pastel hues of laughter's grace,
Whispers echo in this place.

As dusk arrives, the sadness creeps,
Heart's canvas where the sorrow seeps.
Shades of blue in twilight's hold,
Stories of grief quietly told.

Amidst the storm, resilience grows,
Every tear a seed that sows.
In the night, hope's ember glows,
A mosaic, where life flows.

Through every shade, we learn to cope,
In this art, we find our hope.
Each emotion, a brushstroke fine,
Creating the masterpiece of time.

Stars Falling into the Liquid Night

Stars descend like silver tears,
Whispering dreams beneath our fears.
Gliding down with gentle grace,
They leave their light, a warm embrace.

The night unfolds its velvet cloak,
Embers dance, as shadows spoke.
Ripples form on darkened ponds,
Reflecting wishes, timeless bonds.

In liquid night, the world stands still,
Hearts align with nature's will.
Each glimmer maps a hidden chance,
Inviting souls to dream and dance.

As dawn awakes, the stars retreat,
Their secrets held in morning's greet.
Yet in our hearts, they always stay,
Guiding us through night and day.

The Interplay of Light and Shadow

Sunbeams weave through branches bare,
Dancing softly in the air.
Shadow shapes that twist and bend,
Nature's art, a transient trend.

Flickers of light on leaves so green,
Creating sights we've rarely seen.
Darkness lingers, whispers low,
In its depths, bright secrets grow.

The balance shifts with every breath,
Life's a cycle, dance with death.
Every shadow, a tale concealed,
Every light, a truth revealed.

In harmony, they touch and play,
Guiding us through night and day.
Together they create the frame,
Of existence, in beauty's name.

Hearts Adrift on Blessings' Wind

Floating softly, hearts take flight,
Carried forth by winds so light.
Blessings swirl like autumn leaves,
In nature's grasp, the spirit believes.

Breath of spring, a tender sigh,
Promises made in the bright sky.
Every moment, a gift divine,
Gratitude flows like ancient wine.

Through storms that test our weary will,
We find the strength and courage still.
Hearts adrift on love's embrace,
In every trial, we find our place.

With every gust, a hope renewed,
A journey shared, a friendship pursued.
In the dance of life, we spin and glide,
Hearts adrift, with blessings as our guide.

Storms Beneath the Calm

Beneath the quiet skies there lies,
A tempest brewing, masked by sighs.
The winds may whisper soft and low,
Yet shadows gather, fears may grow.

A hidden force of restless might,
Concealed behind the fading light.
The heart knows well the storm's embrace,
In silence dwells a fierce race.

Like thunder rumbles, deep and bold,
A tale of strife yet to unfold.
In every calm, a battle stored,
For in the quiet, storms are poured.

Thus heed the signs, the subtle shift,
In perfect peace, the dark may drift.
For storms beneath the calm reside,
With every wave, the truth will bide.

Heartbeats in the Crash of Waves

The ocean roars, a fierce ballet,
Each wave a pulse, a wild play.
In rhythm with the heart's own beats,
A dance of life, where silence meets.

Waves crash hard against the shore,
A symphony of wanting more.
In salty air, the heart does rise,
As echoes mingle with the skies.

Upon the tides, our dreams are cast,
In fleeting moments, shadows passed.
And in each swell, we find our way,
To breathe in love, and dare to stay.

So listen close, where water flows,
In every crest, the essence grows.
For heartbeats join the waves' embrace,
An endless rhythm we must face.

Mapping the Depths of Care

In ink of kindness, lines are drawn,
Each mark a token of the dawn.
The cartographer of gentle hearts,
In every act, compassion starts.

With tender strokes, the map unfolds,
Through winding paths, a journey told.
For every care, a depth to find,
A sea of love, where we're entwined.

Beneath the surface, currents flow,
Invisible threads of warmth we sow.
In deep connections, trust is layered,
The heart's true map, always favored.

So let us chart this vast expanse,
With every heartbeat, take a chance.
In mapping depths, we weave the thread,
Of bonds unbroken, life well bred.

Floating on the Surface of Grief

A gentle wave, the memory calls,
In tears that glisten, silence falls.
We float upon this fragile sea,
Where pain and love are bound to be.

The heart may ache, yet still it beats,
A dance of sorrow, bittersweet.
In every crest, a whisper stays,
An echo of our fleeting days.

Yet hope remains beneath the tide,
Where sorrow's weight, we must abide.
With every breath, we rise and sink,
In spaces vast, we learn to think.

So let the waters wash away,
The heaviness, the words unsaid.
For floating gently on this grief,
Brings solace to the heart's belief.

Echoes in the Salt-Kissed Air

Waves whisper tales of yore,
Songs of mariners and lore.
The sea breeze carries the past,
And moments ebbing fast.

Seagulls dance on the breeze,
A fluid grace, hearts ease.
Footprints fade on the shore,
Where memories linger more.

Shells hold secrets, not in vain,
Each one etched with time's reign.
Salt-kissed air sharp and bright,
Guides the lost to the light.

In the twilight's gentle glow,
Echoes of laughter flow.
Under stars, dreams comply,
As the ocean waves sigh.

Sailing Through Emotional Tempests

Winds howl, and the thunder rolls,
Heart's compass, it wavers and tolls.
The sea's rage mirrors my fears,
In the storm, I drown my tears.

Sails billow high, hopes collide,
Navigating tides, I can't hide.
Every wave, a piercing scream,
Lost in the tempest's dream.

Yet within chaos, I find a light,
An anchor rock, holding tight.
Through squalls, my spirit will rise,
Guided by love's lullabies.

As the horizon breaks anew,
I find strength to sail through.
With each gust, I learn to steer,
Facing tempests without fear.

The Quietude of Unrushed Waters

In the stillness, ripples play,
Time slows; it's a gentle sway.
Reflections dance on the lake,
Whispers of peace they make.

Reeds bow low, secrets untold,
Nature's grace, calm and bold.
A soft breeze caresses my face,
Easing my heart to embrace.

Frogs sing softly, stars appear,
Every moment, crystal clear.
Amidst the world's fray and noise,
I find my heart's quiet joys.

Beneath the sky, vast and wide,
In tranquil waters, I abide.
Resting here, I feel the flow,
In the silence, I learn to grow.

A Crest of Joy, A Trough of Pain

Life unfolds in waves we ride,
Moments swell, then subside.
Heights of joy, depths of despair,
In this ocean, love lays bare.

Crests cradle laughter's song,
While troughs reveal where we belong.
Every tear, a fleeting trace,
Each smile, a warm embrace.

The dance of joy, a fleeting fawn,
Yet in shadows, we are drawn.
Embrace the ebb, the flow, the gain,
For joy is bright, and pain is rain.

Through it all, we learn to stand,
With open hearts and steady hands.
A journey rich in every hue,
In every crest, love rings true.

The Whispering Ocean

Waves crash softly on the sand,
Secrets held in gentle hands.
Voices call from depths below,
Echoes linger, ebb and glow.

Moonlight dances on the tide,
Every ripple, whisper wide.
Tales of sailors long since passed,
In the ocean's heart amassed.

Seagulls cry with distant grace,
Nature's song in endless space.
With each pulse, the water sighs,
Carrying dreams beneath the skies.

In the stillness, moments freeze,
The ocean's breath, a soft tease.
Listen close, the stories start,
The whispering ocean speaks to the heart.

Flowing Through Shadows

In the forest, where light wanes,
Whispers echo through the lanes.
Shadows dance and stories blend,
A hidden path that seems to bend.

Trees stand tall, their branches twine,
Caressing air, a secret sign.
Beneath the leaves, the silence grows,
A river flows where no one knows.

Footsteps soft on earthy ground,
In the quiet, peace is found.
Nature breathes, a solemn guide,
Through the shadows, dreams reside.

As the twilight beckons near,
The world whispers, full of cheer.
Flowing through this sacred space,
Life unfolds at its own pace.

Raindrops of Reminiscence

Raindrops fall upon the pane,
Each a memory, sweet refrain.
Pitter-patter, soft and clear,
Whispers from the past draw near.

In their dance, they weave a tale,
Fragments caught in silver veil.
Every droplet, a fleeting thought,
In their essence, solace sought.

Clouds embrace the evening sky,
As the shadows softly lie.
With each splash, the heart will stir,
Raindrops holding dreams that were.

They remind us of days gone by,
Moments cherished, whispered sigh.
In the rain, a gentle kiss,
Raindrops weave what we might miss.

The Deep Blue Within

Beneath the waves, a world unknown,
Mysteries in silence grown.
Coral reefs and fish that play,
In the deep blue, dreams sway.

A tranquil realm of whispered peace,
In the depths, where worries cease.
Light filters through in spectral hues,
Painting stories we can choose.

Diving down where secrets lie,
Facing fears, we learn to fly.
In the quiet, heartbeats swell,
The deep blue sings, a siren's spell.

Embrace the ocean's vast expanse,
In its depths, take a chance.
Find yourself in waters free,
The deep blue within, harmony.

Reflections on Water's Edge

Gentle ripples kiss the shore,
Mirroring skies forevermore.
Sand clings softly to bare feet,
Where land and liquid softly meet.

Clouds drift by, a fleeting dream,
As sunlight paints the water's gleam.
Whispers echo in the breeze,
Tales of heart, of time, of ease.

Footprints vanish, tides reclaim,
Nature's cycle, all the same.
In tranquil moments, thoughts arise,
Reflections caught in nature's eyes.

Dancers in the Moonlight's Wake

Underneath the silver glow,
Waves sway gently, ebb and flow.
Shadows move with grace and care,
Whispers linger in the air.

Stars above in velvet cloak,
A world alive, a song bespoke.
Couples meet where waters twirl,
Hearts unite, their dreams unfurl.

As tides go in and come back out,
Magic swirls without a doubt.
Together lost in moonlit dance,
Embraced by night, they take a chance.

Salty Tears and Sandy Shores

Waves crash down with a thunderous roar,
Salty tears mixed with ocean's core.
Footprints line the dampened sand,
Stories told by nature's hand.

Memories washed in foamy tides,
Where laughter lingers, love abides.
Each grain holds tales, both lost and found,
Echoes of joy, where hearts are bound.

As the sun dips low, colors blaze,
A fleeting moment, a lasting gaze.
On sandy shores, two souls align,
In the vastness, their hearts entwine.

The Ocean's Canvas of Emotion

Colors swirl in brilliant hues,
The ocean breathes, a canvas views.
Brushstrokes woven with the tide,
On this vast expanse, dreams collide.

Waves of sorrow, waves of glee,
In every splash, a memory.
The world reflects in salty mist,
Layers of life that coexist.

Ebb and flow, the heart's own song,
In every ripple, we belong.
Nature's art, a constant theme,
In the ocean's heart, we dream.

Secrets Buried Beneath the Waves

Upon the ocean's breathing tide,
Whispers hide in shadows wide.
Lost tales of those who sailed afar,
Their dreams anchored to a distant star.

Beneath the blue, where shadows creep,
Lies a world that does not sleep.
Coral keeps its ancient lore,
Guarding secrets on the ocean floor.

Waves crash softly on the shore,
Echoes of hearts that yearn for more.
In salty tears and whispered sighs,
History's pulse beneath dark skies.

With each foam-kissed grain of sand,
Stories whisper, grand and bland.
The ocean cradles every dream,
As time dances like a silver beam.

The Shoreline's Gentle Haunting

Footprints left in morning light,
Waves erase them from our sight.
Yet the shoreline calls to me,
In its voice, a haunting plea.

Shells and pebbles, stories old,
Guard the dreams of sailors bold.
Each whisper in the salty breeze,
Tells of love and memories.

The tide retreats, as if to say,
We must hold on, yet drift away.
Ghostly ships that sail the night,
Fading softly from our sight.

Underneath a silver sky,
The echoes linger, never die.
In every wave and grain of sand,
The shoreline's secret we can't understand.

Eclipsed by Love's Swell

In twilight's glow, two shadows blend,
A dance of hearts, where dreams transcend.
The ocean swells with whispered tones,
Love's embrace like ancient stones.

Rising tides and falling stars,
Tell the tale of loves from afar.
Each gentle wave, a soft caress,
In love's eclipse, we find our rest.

As moonlight skims the rippling sea,
Our hearts surrender, wild and free.
With every pulse, the night ignites,
In this realm of endless nights.

Together lost in sailor's lore,
We weave our dreams forevermore.
Eclipsed by time, yet never lost,
In love's great swell, we find the cost.

Echos Resounding in the Stillness

In quiet moments by the shore,
Echos linger, tales of yore.
The waves whisper in soft refrain,
Singing songs of joy and pain.

Each ripple holds a memory,
Of laughter shared, of harmony.
In stillness found beneath the sky,
Echos of love that never die.

Footsteps dance where silence reigns,
Drifting softly through the plains.
The beauty of a wordless song,
In gentle waves, we all belong.

So let the ocean hold our song,
With every tide, we will be strong.
In echoes, felt and understood,
We find solace, we find good.

Echoes on the Shore

Whispers in the salty air,
Footprints washed away with care.
Tides that tell of tales once known,
In moonlit glow, they find their throne.

Seagulls cry, a distant song,
With every wave, they drift along.
Memories dance and fade away,
As sunlight bursts in bright display.

Shells that hold the ocean's dreams,
Reflecting hues of silver gleams.
The beach, a canvas, vast and wide,
Where nature's secrets always hide.

In the rhythm of the sea,
Echoes linger, wild and free.
With every breath, I feel its pull,
A timeless bond that makes me whole.

Drowning in Reflection

A mirror lake, so calm, so deep,
Where thoughts drift softly, secrets keep.
Beneath the surface, shadows sway,
In silence, lost, I choose to stay.

Ripples form with every sigh,
As memories float and gently die.
I dive into a world unknown,
Where fragments of my heart are sewn.

Faces fade, yet echoes ring,
In whispers of the heart, they cling.
Each glance, a tale, alone and raw,
In stillness, I can learn to thaw.

Drowning in the depths I find,
Reflections of a troubled mind.
But in the dark, a light will gleam,
And guide me toward a brighter dream.

Drifting Dreams

On a breeze, my thoughts take flight,
Carried far beyond the night.
Stars above, they hum a tune,
As hopes arise, beneath the moon.

Clouds like ships in endless blue,
Sailing toward horizons new.
In visions soft, my heart will soar,
As dreams unfold on distant shores.

Gentle echoes of the past,
Remind me that these moments last.
With every wave of dusk and dawn,
New journeys start, the old are gone.

Through twilight's veil, I seek the light,
Chasing shadows, taking flight.
With drifting dreams, my spirit roams,
In every heart that finds its home.

The Current of Hearts

Beneath the surface, stories flow,
In currents deep where feelings grow.
A river wide, a tapestry,
Of whispers shared, of you and me.

Each pulse of water carries fate,
In every drop, we intertwine, create.
Together, drifting hand in hand,
Through wild terrains, we learn to stand.

In tidal surges, passions rise,
They crash like waves against the skies.
With every turn, new paths appear,
Our hearts entwined, we conquer fear.

The current runs, relentless, strong,
A melody, our timeless song.
In this embrace, we find our way,
In love's embrace, we choose to stay.

Shimmering Hopes Beneath the Deep

In the depths, where silence dwells,
Shimmering dreams like distant bells.
Each echo whispers of what could be,
Hopes igniting like stars in the sea.

Waves dance gently under moon's grace,
Carrying secrets to a hidden place.
Beneath the surface, life weaves a thread,
A tapestry of all that's unsaid.

Ripples of thought shimmer and sway,
Guiding lost souls on their way.
The ocean's heart beats with might,
Cradling wishes in the night.

In this world, vast and profound,
Shimmering hopes forever abound.
Each heartbeat echoes, fierce and true,
Beneath the deep, dreams renew.

The Crescendo of an Evening Breeze

As dusk unfolds its velvet gown,
The evening breeze whispers all around.
Notes of warmth and promises blend,
A song of twilight that will not end.

Gentle rustles through the trees,
A soothing symphony on the breeze.
Tales untold drift through the air,
Memories linger everywhere.

Stars emerge, a celestial choir,
Igniting the sky, igniting desire.
The crescendo builds, a sweet embrace,
Where time and hope share a space.

In the quiet, hearts align,
Tracing rhythms, tender, divine.
The evening's magic softly weaves,
A lullaby that never leaves.

Beneath the Guise of Tranquility

In stillness lies a hidden tale,
Beneath the calm, emotions sail.
A façade of peace, yet deep inside,
The storms of life unceasingly collide.

Whispers dance on quiet streams,
Masking the chaos that softly screams.
The world outside may seem so bright,
Yet shadows linger just out of sight.

Serenity plays a clever game,
In tranquil pools, we hide our flame.
Yet beneath the calm, a heart beats wild,
Yearning always, untouched and unfiled.

In moments of pause, we find the truth,
That peace is often uncoupled from youth.
The guise of tranquility may deceive,
But every heart still dares to believe.

Navigating Between Heartbeats

In the silence, where time does pause,
Beat by beat, we redefine our cause.
Navigating spaces, both wide and narrow,
Each heartbeat's echo, a fleeting arrow.

Between the moments, life quietly flows,
Connecting the highs and the lows.
In whispered exchanges of breath and sigh,
A dance of souls that will never die.

Listen closely, the rhythm's embrace,
Guides us softly through time and space.
In the heartbeat's pulse, stories reside,
A tapestry woven with love as our guide.

As we journey, hand in hand,
In the spaces between, we understand.
Life's true magic lies not in haste,
But in how we navigate every heartbeat's taste.

Waves of Whispers

Softly the ocean speaks, in hues of blue,
Secrets flow like tides, in a dance that's true.
Echoes of dreams ride high upon the crest,
Cradled in the arms of the sea, we rest.

Gentle caresses, the wind carries sound,
Whispers of ancient worlds, forever unbound.
Each wave a story, a timeless refrain,
Calling the hearts of those lost in the pain.

Moonlit reflections draw us ever near,
Holding our fears like the mist in the pier.
Hope glimmers bright in the depths of despair,
In waves of whispers, we find solace there.

With every break, a new chance to begin,
Waves crash and retreat, where losses have been.
In this vast expanse, we learn to let go,
For life ebbs and flows, as we learn to grow.

Currents of the Heart

In currents unseen, emotions cascade,
Hidden beneath, where dreams silently wade.
Stronger than rivers that carve through the land,
The heart finds solace, in whispers so grand.

Rushing like waters through valleys of strife,
Currents collide, we navigate life.
Moments of chaos, a swirl to embrace,
Each heartbeat a pulse in this intimate space.

Yet calmness prevails in the deep, still unknown,
The heart beats with rhythm, it's never alone.
Connections like streams, flow gentle and bright,
Uniting our souls in the softest of light.

Through joys and sorrows, the currents will shift,
Navigating love, our most precious gift.
With every encounter, we learn and we yearn,
In the dance of the heart, there's always a return.

Ebb and Flow of Emotion

Like tides we rise and fall, through joy and despair,
The ebb and flow of emotion, a constant affair.
Moments of laughter, drowned in the night,
Shadows retreat, as morning brings light.

The heart swells with waves, of anger and pain,
Yet washes away, like the soft summer rain.
Each swell a reminder of what we hold dear,
The ebb and flow whispers, to always be near.

Receding like sunset, in dusk's tender glow,
The whispering winds teach us how to let go.
In stillness, we find the strength to believe,
That emotions, like oceans, are here to receive.

Closeness and distance, they dance in our soul,
Ebbing and flowing, to make us whole.
In this timeless rhythm, we come to know,
The beauty of change in life's endless flow.

Celestial Pulls

Underneath the stars, we feel their embrace,
Celestial pulls guide us through endless space.
Gravity of dreams, like planets we chase,
Navigating darkness, we roam with grace.

The moon's tender glow, a beacon so bright,
Shining on paths forged in the still of the night.
Forgotten wishes, like comets that fly,
We reach for the cosmos, as our spirits cry.

In constellations, our stories unfold,
A tapestry woven with threads of the bold.
Each star a promise, each planet a song,
In the dance of the heavens, we all belong.

We drift among galaxies, where wonders abound,
In the symphony of stars, our hearts resonate sound.
Celestial pulls remind us we're free,
United in starlight, you and me.

Fragmented Reflections at Dusk

Shadows stretch across the ground,
Whispers of the light abound.
Colors bleed into the night,
Fragmented dreams take flight.

Memories dance like fireflies,
Glimmers in the evening skies.
Each thought a hint of what's to be,
In twilight's gentle reverie.

Fading echoes fill the air,
Scattered pieces linger there.
With every heartbeat, time will wane,
Yet still we yearn for what remains.

The dusk envelops all we know,
An enigma in its glow.
In this space where shadows blend,
We find beginnings in the end.

A Sea of Uncharted Sentiments

Waves of feelings rise and fall,
Drifting echoes, nature's call.
Hearts adrift on tides unknown,
Seeking solace, feeling alone.

Currents pull at dreams untold,
Stories buried, yet so bold.
Sailing forth through starry night,
Guided by the moon's soft light.

Boats of hope on azure seas,
Yearning whispers in the breeze.
Navigating through the storm,
Finding warmth in the forlorn.

Anchored deep in thoughts we share,
Souls entwined in tranquil prayer.
In unison, we chart our fate,
On this sea where hearts await.

Castaways in an Emotional Bay

Stranded on this lonely shore,
Tides of longing, evermore.
Echoes of a heart's refrain,
Castaways in joy and pain.

Drifting boats with sails unfurled,
Hopes and fears collide in whirl.
Memories washed upon the sand,
Time slips through like grains so grand.

Together here, we search for peace,
Finding solace, piece by piece.
Among the waves, we learn to trust,
In this bay of love and dust.

Open skies above us gleam,
Beneath the stars, we dare to dream.
Swordfish swim through our abyss,
Guiding us to the heart of bliss.

The Calm Before the Crashing Wave

Stillness rests upon the sea,
Whispers hold what's yet to be.
Breath of wind, a silent plea,
The calm before, the storm is free.

Tension builds in azure space,
Nature stirs with quiet grace.
Hearts anticipate the swell,
Eager for the tale to tell.

Moments pause, the sun dips low,
In this hush, the feelings grow.
Yet beneath the tranquil face,
The waves lie in their fierce embrace.

When the crash at last will come,
In the thunder, we drum.
For every calm brings forth the fight,
In love's tempest, we find light.

Ebb and Flow of Silent Echoes

Whispers fade in twilight's grip,
Softly spoken, shadows slip.
Ripples dance in quiet streams,
Echoes fade, lost in dreams.

Time meanders, secrets held,
In the silence, hearts have swelled.
Waves recede, the shore grows bare,
Silent stories linger there.

Underneath the crescent glow,
Memories like water flow.
Each heartbeat a distant call,
Ebb and flow, we rise and fall.

In twilight's embrace we find,
The echoes left behind,
In the stillness, we may know,
Life's soft rhythm, ebb and flow.

Currents of Unspoken Longing

Beneath the surface, tides collide,
Words unspoken, feelings hide.
A longing slips through veiled intent,
In silence, dreams are often spent.

The heart beats in secret tones,
In shadows cast, it softly moans.
Currents pull, a silent plea,
In the depths, it longs to be.

Eyes meet like waves in the night,
Unvoiced wishes take their flight.
Underneath the stars we chase,
Currents whisper, find our place.

In the depths, a spark ignites,
Through the darkness, love ignites.
Unspoken words, they gently flow,
Carried on the undertow.

A Driftwood's Soliloquy

Washed ashore on sandy dreams,
A driftwood speaks in silent streams.
Whispers echo ancient tales,
Of journeys seized by wind and gales.

Stranded but not lost, it sighs,
Underneath the open skies.
Each knot a story, each bend a choice,
In solitude, it finds its voice.

Time etches lines upon its frame,
Weathered and worn, still the same.
Through storms endured, it stands so tall,
A testament to rise after fall.

In the twilight, shadows creep,
As the ocean's secrets sleep.
A driftwood's heart with tales to weave,
In the silence, it believes.

The Rhythm of Emotional Currents

In the heart's depths, currents flow,
Emotions rise, then fade, then grow.
Like ocean tides at break of dawn,
A dance begins, and then it's gone.

The pulse of love, a steady beat,
In whispered moments, bittersweet.
Feelings crash, then softly rest,
Carried by waves, we are blessed.

Each rhythm tells a story true,
A melody for me and you.
Like river bends, our paths entwined,
In every current, life defined.

Emotional waves, they ebb and flow,
Guided by winds we do not know.
Together lost, together found,
In the rhythm, we are bound.

The Undulating Soul

In the quiet depths it sways,
A rhythm lost in time's embrace.
Waves of thought in gentle play,
Seeking peace, a sacred space.

Ebb and flow of hopes and fears,
Tides that whisper through the night.
Carrying dreams like fragile spheres,
Floating softly toward the light.

In the stillness, hearts unfold,
Yearning for the skies above.
Stories of the brave and bold,
Written on the waves of love.

Rising up, the spirit flies,
Above the depths where shadows dwell.
In the dance beneath the skies,
The soul's sweet song begins to swell.

Storms Beneath the Surface

Beneath calm waters, tempests brew,
Whispers echo of the fight.
Hidden struggles, raw and true,
Beneath the calm, the storm ignites.

Clouds of doubt, they churn and rise,
Lightning flashes, fears align.
Yet in chaos, wisdom lies,
A strength to conquer, truly mine.

Rages dance, a fierce ballet,
As thunder rolls with mighty sound.
In each pulse, old wounds give way,
New resilience shall be found.

Emerging from the winds' embrace,
A clearer path comes into view.
With each trial, I find my place,
Storms beneath, I'll journey through.

Shifting Sands of Thought

Thoughts like grains beneath my feet,
Shifting with each passing breeze.
Some are bitter, some are sweet,
Carried gently by the seas.

Tides of change sweep through the land,
Waves of doubt and waves of trust.
Each new idea, like a strand,
Weaves a future, bright and just.

In the desert, whispers call,
Voices lost in sunlit haze.
Yet a wisdom beckons all,
Guiding through the shifting days.

From the cacophony of noise,
A clear vision starts to form.
In the silence, I rejoice,
New horizons, bright and warm.

Cascades of Joy

Like waterfalls in morning light,
Joy cascades, a brilliant show.
Dancing droplets, pure and bright,
Each one sparkles, warm aglow.

In the laughter, echoes ring,
Celebrating life's sweet song.
Moments cherished, hearts take wing,
In this flow, where we belong.

Through the valleys, joy will flow,
Filling spaces left by pain.
In the currents, love will glow,
Washing over, like soft rain.

So let the rivers freely run,
Let joy's whispers guide the way.
In the warmth of life's sweet sun,
Hearts find hope in every day.

Undercurrents of Desire

Whispers in the twilight air,
Flickering shadows, a hidden stare.
Pulse of the night, soft and wary,
Hearts entwined, sweet and scary.

Secrets dance in moonlit nights,
A flame ignites, ignites the sights.
Tides of passion, gentle and bold,
Stories of warmth yet to be told.

Beneath the surface, dreams reside,
Yearnings deep, we cannot hide.
Embers glow in the silence shared,
In the currents, we are bared.

With each heartbeat, time unveils,
In the depths, our spirit sails.
Undercurrents, soft and true,
Together lost, yet found anew.

Melodies of the Mind

Echoes linger in the night,
Thoughts like stars, they take flight.
Harmonies weave in silence deep,
Awakening dreams from their sleep.

Notes of wisdom softly gleam,
In the solitude, we find our theme.
Universes inside us play,
Guiding shadows through the fray.

Timeless rhythms make us whole,
Symphonies arise, soothing the soul.
In the quiet, clarity flows,
Revealing hidden paths that show.

Every heartbeat sings its song,
In the mind, where we belong.
Melodies merge into life's design,
Each thought a thread, perfectly aligned.

Surges of Longing

Waves crash softly on the shore,
Each retreat pulls at the core.
Yearnings rise with the crescent moon,
Time stands still, a haunting tune.

Fingers trace the salty air,
Whispers of hope, dreams laid bare.
In the distance, a faint call,
A longing heart that mustn't fall.

Underneath the starry skies,
Visions dance, and spirits rise.
Surges come, relentless tide,
In their depths, our souls abide.

Beneath the tempest of our hearts,
Fragments of us never part.
Each surge carries tales unspoken,
In desire's wake, we are broken.

The Sea Within Us

Beneath our skin, the ocean breathes,
Tides of feelings, it gently weaves.
In every pulse, the waves obey,
The sea within, it charts the way.

Currents rush through veins so strong,
A dance of life, where we belong.
Mysteries swirl in depths unknown,
In this water, we find our home.

Sands of time drift through our grasp,
Moments fleeting, we cherish fast.
In storms we find our strength to grow,
The sea within us, forever flows.

Each drop of rain, each whispering breeze,
Connects our souls with tender ease.
As we dive deep into the night,
The sea within guides us to light.

Navigating the Abyss

In shadows deep, where silence reigns,
A journey starts, through unseen chains.
The echoes call, in haunting tones,
Each step reveals the heart of stones.

With lantern light, I pierce the night,
The fears I face ignite the fight.
In every whisper, courage grows,
Through labyrinths, a path that flows.

The void's embrace can shatter dreams,
Yet from the dark, a brave heart beams.
I rise again, from depths I've known,
For in the abyss, strength is grown.

Through trials faced, I find my way,
Navigating the night to day.
Each tear that falls, a lesson learned,
In the heart of darkness, light is burned.

The Rhythm of Raindrops

Softly they fall, like tears from skies,
A melody sweet, where nature sighs.
Each drop a note, in whispers clear,
A symphony sung for all to hear.

They dance on leaves, in playful grace,
Creating art in every space.
The world awakes, in gentle tunes,
As raindrops play beneath the moons.

They kiss the earth with tender care,
Each splash a story, rich and rare.
In puddles formed, reflections gleam,
They weave together, life's simple dream.

A rhythm born from nature's heart,
In every drop, a work of art.
So let us listen, feel the song,
In the rhythm of raindrops, we belong.

Whispers of the Ocean's Heart

In twilight's glow, the waves do speak,
With secrets old, they softly leak.
A lullaby of tides and dreams,
In whispers soft, the ocean gleams.

The breeze carries tales from afar,
Of sunken ships and distant stars.
Each crest a voice, each trough a sigh,
In salty air, the memories lie.

The sand holds footprints, stories told,
Of lovers' vows and hearts of gold.
With every ebb, with every flow,
The ocean's heart begins to show.

So linger long, by waters deep,
Embrace the words that ocean keeps.
In every wave, a verse will start,
A timeless echo of the heart.

Waves of Forgotten Dreams

On shores of time, where shadows dwell,
Lie dreams once bright, now hard to tell.
They rise like tides, then fade away,
In whispers lost, they yearn to stay.

Each crash of surf, a story lost,
Of hopes once held, at tender cost.
Yet in the mist, a glimmer shines,
A chance to weave new lifelines.

The horizon calls, with colors bold,
A canvas wide, where hearts unfold.
Embrace the waves, let go the fear,
For every dream, the ocean hears.

From depths unknown, new visions bloom,
In currents deep, dispelling gloom.
With every swell, I rise and claim,
A tapestry of hope, not shame.

The Serenade of Distant Shores

The wind whispers soft and low,
As waves dance under the moon's glow.
Voices of sailors from afar,
Sing tales of love beneath the stars.

With every crest, a heartbeat sings,
Echoes of freedom the ocean brings.
The distant shores call out to me,
In dreams forever, I long to be.

From cliffs so high, the view enchants,
Seagulls circle and the horizon grants.
A melody written in the deep,
Where secrets of the sea shall keep.

In the twilight's embrace, I stand,
A serenade sung over the sand.
The night unfolds its mystic lore,
While I am lost in the distant shore.

Secrets of the Moonlit Bay

Beneath the sky, the waters gleam,
A tapestry of silver dream.
Whispers float upon the tide,
Secrets where the shadows slide.

Crickets sing a soft refrain,
Their music mingles with the rain.
In the hush of night, hearts connect,
Bound by the magic we protect.

The moon casts spells on every wave,
A guardian for the brave.
In this bay, we leave our fears,
And share our hopes through silent tears.

In the stillness, time stands still,
Each moment wrapped in a gentle thrill.
The secrets of the night unfold,
In the moonlit bay, our tales are told.

The Confluence of Memory and Hope

In twilight's haze, the past retreats,
While future echoes gently beats.
Memories dance like leaves in flight,
In the confluence of day and night.

Faded smiles and laughter shared,
In every heart, a love declared.
Hope rises with the morning sun,
Reminding us that we are one.

Along the river, shadows play,
Where time touches what will stay.
Each stream a story, flowing free,
Of what was lost and yet to be.

In this space, we find our way,
With every thought, a bridge we lay.
The confluence flows with strength and grace,
Binding our dreams in this sacred place.

Sheltered in the Arms of Waves

Cradled gently, the ocean sighs,
As soft tides whisper lullabies.
In the embrace of foamy crest,
I find my soul at peace, at rest.

The horizon stretches, vast and wide,
A sanctuary where dreams abide.
Every ripple, a memory made,
In the arms of waves that softly fade.

Each surge carries a tale to share,
Of sun-drenched days and love laid bare.
Sheltered here, my fears subside,
As the sea wraps me like a guiding tide.

Beneath the stars, my spirit soars,
With whispered secrets from the shores.
In nature's bosom, I find my place,
Sheltered in waves, a warm embrace.

Erosion of Time on Emotional Beaches

Waves crash softly, whispers of loss,
Footprints washed away, a heavy cost.
The shoreline shifts, memories bend,
Each grain of sand, a story to send.

Tides recede, revealing the past,
Echoes linger, too sweet to last.
Seagulls cry above, tales to narrate,
As the sun sets, we contemplate.

Bleached bones of dreams, scattered and worn,
In the twilight glow, new hopes are born.
Yet the ocean's pull never relents,
Stealing our moments, the heart laments.

Time is a thief on these emotional shores,
Collecting our secrets, opening doors.
Yet every tide brings a chance to be free,
Embracing the ebb, we learn how to see.

Lighthouses of Forgotten Affection

Amidst the fog, their beams still shine,
Guiding lost souls down memory's line.
Forgotten whispers in the wind's soft sigh,
A beacon of love, though days pass by.

Stone towers stand strong against the night,
Holding the warmth of a love once bright.
The light flickers on, a ghostly embrace,
Reminding us still of a long-lost face.

Waves crash below, their song bittersweet,
While inside us lie memories discreet.
Each flash of light tells a tale of old,
Of promises made and of hearts consoled.

In the quiet dusk, we stare at the sea,
Finding our solace, where we used to be.
Though time may dim them, those lighthouses glow,
Illuminating paths only the heart knows.

The Siren's Call of Distant Memories

A haunting melody drifts through the air,
Urging us back to a time filled with care.
In the shadows of dreams, they beckon and plead,
The siren's call, a compelling need.

Footsteps echo on cobblestone streets,
Of laughter and love, time endlessly repeats.
But just as we grasp, they slip from our hands,
Fleeting glimpses of forgotten lands.

Fragile as glass, yet heavy with weight,
These memories linger, intertwining fate.
A song of the past, sweet yet forlorn,
An ache in the heart for what could have worn.

In the twilight haze, we yearn to embrace,
The stories of old, the ghost of a face.
Waves of remembrance crash on the shore,
The siren's call pulling us back evermore.

Driftwood Dreams and Ephemeral Moments

On sandy shores, driftwood does lie,
Carved by the sea, under a vast sky.
Each piece, a story, each knot, a tale,
Of journeys embarked and the winds that sail.

Ephemeral moments like mist in the morn,
Slip through our fingers, fragile and worn.
Yet in their beauty, we find our release,
As time weaves its tapestry, threadbare with peace.

A dance with the waves, we twirl in delight,
Chasing the shadows, lost in the light.
Embracing the now, with hearts open wide,
Finding solace in each ebbing tide.

Though driftwood may fade, and moments may flee,
They shape our essence, they set us free.
For life is a canvas of dreams intertwined,
In the flow of the sea, love's treasures we find.

Shifting Sands of Memory

Whispers drift across the dunes,
Echoes of laughter, soft tunes.
Footprints fade beneath the sun,
Moments lost, yet never done.

Winds that tell a tale of old,
In the silence, dreams unfold.
Each grain holds a story near,
A dance of joy, a trace of fear.

Time flows like a river's bend,
Carrying what we can't amend.
In the twilight, shadows play,
Where memories find their way.

Sands will shift but hearts will stay,
In the depths of yesterday.
Always yearning, always bold,
In this timeless dance, behold.

Under the Surface of Serenity

Beneath the calm, the waves conceal,
A world where silence starts to heal.
Gentle ripples, whispers low,
Secrets only the heart can know.

Luminous depths, shadows glide,
In stillness, spirits dance inside.
Moments linger, soft and bright,
In harmony, they take their flight.

The surface glistens, peace invokes,
While undercurrents swirl like smoke.
A tranquil mask, a hidden tide,
Where inner storms and calm collide.

Serenity holds, yet guides away,
To places where truth yearns to sway.
In the quiet, dreams arise,
Revealing depths, the soul's disguise.

Flowing Through the Heart's Estuary

In the estuary, emotions meet,
Currents pulse beneath our feet.
Tides of longing, waves of grace,
A dance of love in space embraced.

Rippling waters, stories blend,
Carried forth where pathways bend.
Fragments drifting, moments blend,
In this flow, we find our end.

Colors swirl in twilight's hue,
Every hue a dream anew.
Hearts beat softly, side by side,
In the estuary, we confide.

Life matters where the rivers cross,
In this confluence, we find loss.
Yet flowing free, we learn to fly,
As love grows deep, we touch the sky.

The Pull of Celestial Bodies

Stars align in the midnight sky,
A cosmic dance as time slips by.
Gravity's thread holds hearts so tight,
In the dark, we seek the light.

Planets spin in a silent tune,
Guiding dreams beneath the moon.
From afar, a gentle call,
Echoes softly, binding all.

Asteroids whisper through the void,
Moments cherished, love deployed.
In quantum leaps, emotions soar,
A gravity we can't ignore.

Celestial tides draw us near,
In starry night, hopes disappear.
Yet in the pull, we find our place,
In this vast, endless embrace.

Glimmers of Love's Reflection

In twilight's soft embrace we dwell,
With whispers sweet, our secrets swell.
Like stars that blink in midnight air,
Your gaze ignites a fervent flare.

Through gardens lush and dreams untold,
Our hearts entwined, a warmth to hold.
Each moment shared, a shimmering thread,
In love's reflection, softly spread.

With laughter bright, we chase the night,
In each other's arms, everything feels right.
A dance of souls beneath the skies,
In glimmers bright, our spirit flies.

Together we sail on oceans wide,
No fear of storms when you're my guide.
In love's embrace, we find our way,
With glimmers shining, come what may.

Ephemeral Waves of Joy

In fleeting moments, laughter sparkles,
Like sunlight dancing on the ripples.
Each wave that crashes fades away,
Yet in our hearts, those echoes stay.

With every smile, a memory blooms,
Filling our world with sweet perfumes.
We chase the tides, unburdened, free,
In joyful waves, just you and me.

The winds may change, the skies may gray,
But joy remains, come what may.
In every heartbeat, a spark remains,
In ephemeral waves, love never wanes.

We surf the moments, wild and bright,
In the dance of joy, we find our light.
With every breath, we rise and fall,
In fleeting joy, we have it all.

The Abyss of Longing's Depth

In shadows deep, my heart does yearn,
For traces left, for love's return.
Each sigh a whisper of your name,
In longing's chasm, burning flame.

With every tear a story told,
Of dreams once bright, now dimmed and cold.
The night is endless, silence loud,
In the abyss, I call your shroud.

Stars above, they seem to mock,
The emptiness, the endless clock.
Yet in the dark, I hold a spark,
A flicker bright against the stark.

For love is fierce, even in pain,
Through deepest sorrow, hope will reign.
In longing's depth, I'll find my way,
Until that dawn breaks into day.

Heartstrings Beneath the Riptide

In turbulent seas where shadows play,
Our heartstrings tugged in tides' ballet.
Beneath the waves, our souls entwine,
In currents deep, your heart is mine.

With each pull, I feel the ache,
Of love's sweet song, a careful make.
Though riptides roar and tempests cry,
In love's embrace, we learn to fly.

Through tidal storms, our bond will grow,
In depths of chaos, love will flow.
Found in the whirlpool's fierce embrace,
Heartstrings connect, in time and space.

Together we've faced the stormy high,
In swirling depths, we dare defy.
With heartstrings strong, we'll brave the tide,
For love's embrace, our faithful guide.

Milton Keynes UK
Ingram Content Group UK Ltd.
UKHW052021251024
450245UK00012B/627